FUN BALLOONS
With G & Gigi

Their first business story.

Written and illustrated by Alejandro Rodriguez

(Photo Album Edition)

G was a good listener.

G's dad rewarded him, and they went to the Balloon Land store to get one balloon:

G chose a kit of fun balloons.

They spent time as a family learning how to make them and made a bunch.

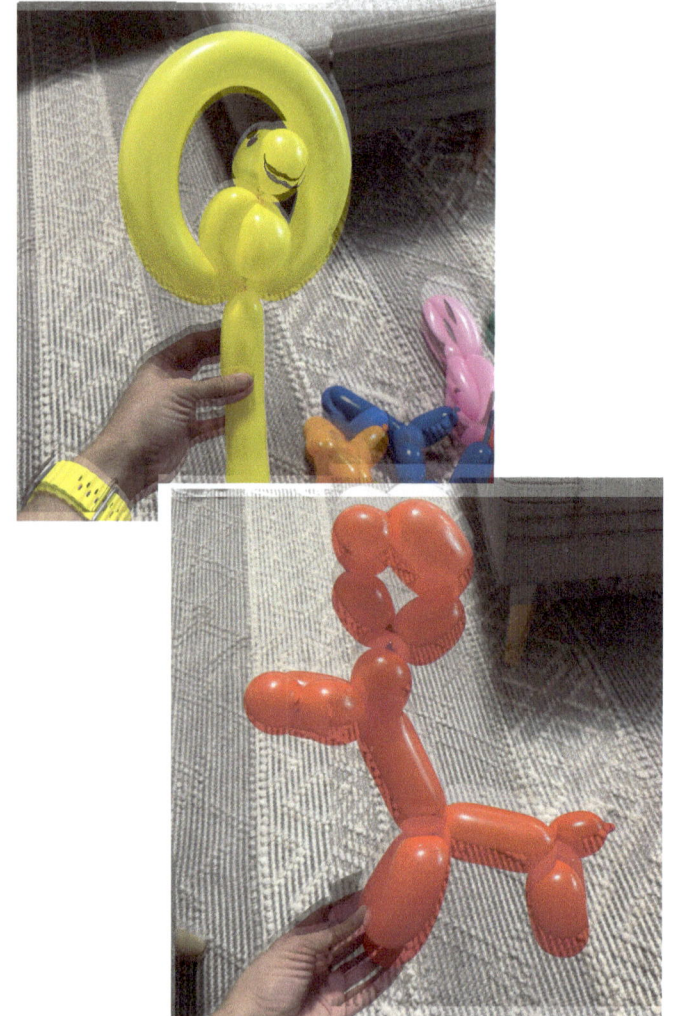

They were so fun and colorful!

G was having fun and gathered all the balloons in a basket!

G's dad said, "You have so many balloons. You can sell them!"

G loved the idea and got his sister Gigi excited about it.

Their dad brought a table, two stools, paper, marker, tape, scissors, and a cup for the money.

The first thing they did was create a sign to let their customers know what their business was about. So they named it "Fun Balloons 25 ¢".

G & Gigi started putting some balloons on the side of the table to show everyone how fun and colorful they were!

And just like that, they were open for business!

At first, they were just sitting there. Cars would pass by, but no one would stop. They remember to be patient.

A man running towards them catches their attention, and Gigi looks at him with a smile while G becomes shy.

The man shouts, "Sorry, I don't have cash, but I will come back!

G gets sad, but Gigi reminds him to have fun!

They both started waving their hands and shouting, "We are open for business!" They are having Fun!

All of a sudden, a car stops by. Could this be it?

"Hello! what are you two selling today?" She asks.

G said, "Hello! We are selling fun balloons!"

And just like that, they had their first client and made their first sale for $5!

Then they had a second customer!

And a third one! The business was working!

G & Gigi made their customers very happy by treating them with much love, gratitude, and respect! They would say things like Hello & Welcome! How is your day? My pleasure! Thank you! God Bless you!

Everyone loved their
Fun balloons!

G & Gigi worked great as a team! Not only when they were with customers.

But also when they were by themselves.

Their first business was a total hit, and G & Gigi had many awesome clients!

And just like that, after meeting great people, they Sold Out!

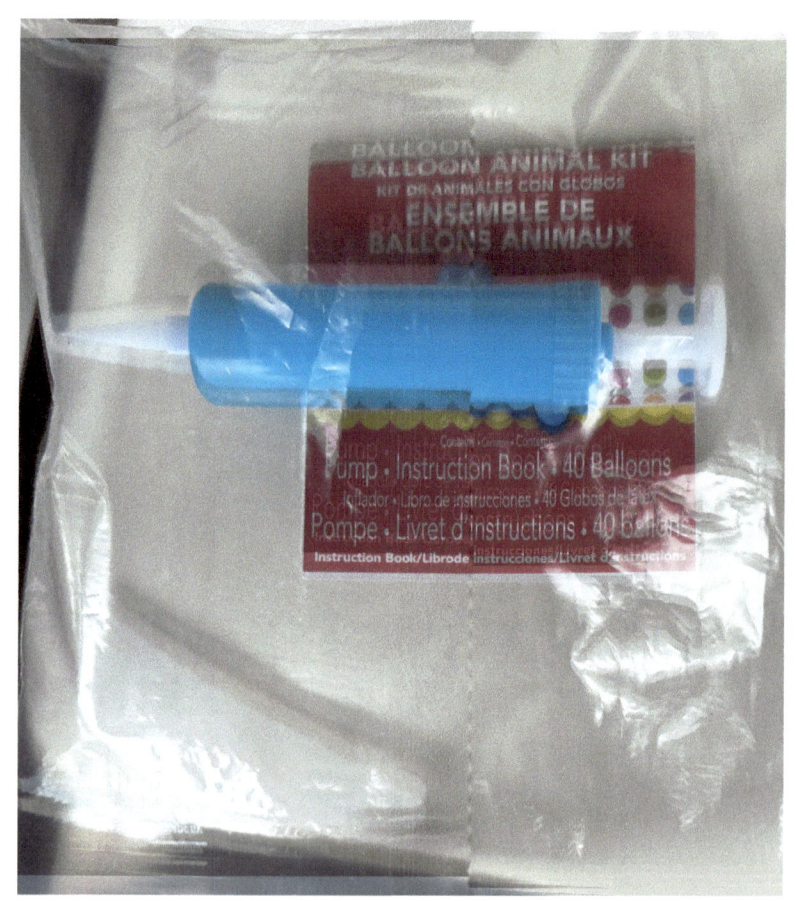

G & Gigi sold all 40 balloons, well, a few of them popped, but that is ok and part of doing business.

G saved one balloon for the guy who told him he would be back. G waited for him, but he never returned, and G felt sad.

G's dad noticed G was sad and said, let's just hope he made it home ok; maybe he forgot like silly Papa forgets things too.

They both laugh, and G's dad gets a friendly reminder of how important it is to keep our word and its impact on others.

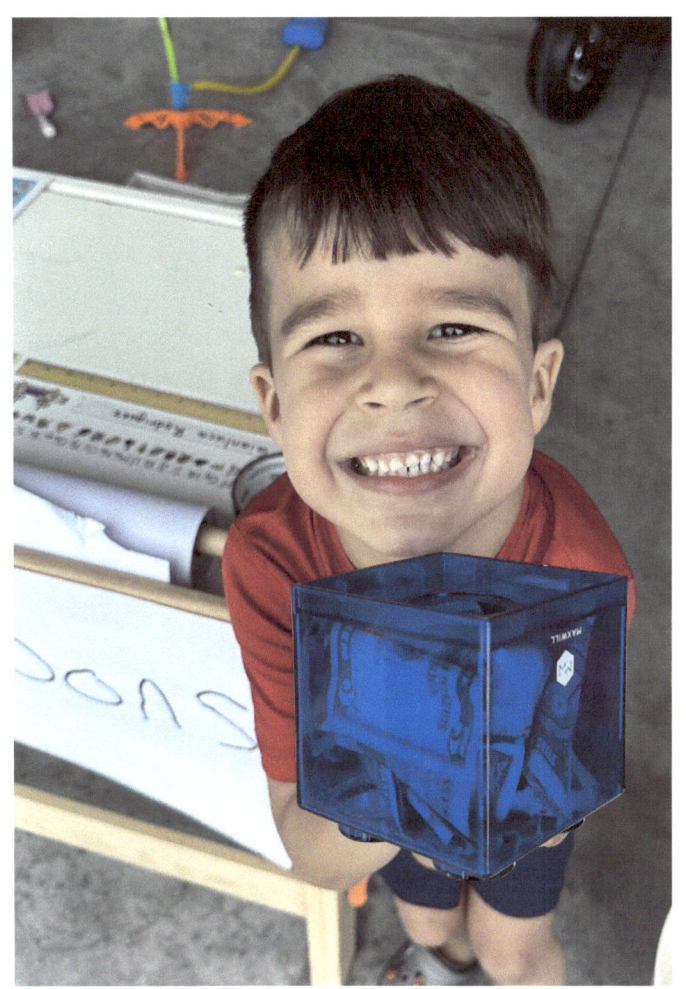

G & Gigi were very grateful!
They had a successful day!

They counted their money and made $31!

More important than money, G & Gigi had a great time together, created fun memories, and met awesome supportive neighbors!

G & Gigi invites you to give a Fun Balloons business a try with the help and permission of your parents!

It's Fun, and you get to learn about the importance of teamwork, patience, community, and keeping your word.

If you decide to have one, send us pictures at a@therods.co. We would love to see it!

A Gift For You!

Download some awesome resources by visiting therods.co/fb

Copyright © 2023 by Alejandro Rodriguez

All rights reserved.

No part of this publication may be reproduced, distributed, or transmitted in any form or by any means, including photocopying, recording, or other electronic or mechanical methods, without the prior written permission of the publisher, except as permitted by U.S. copyright law. For permission requests, contact a@therods.co

Written and illustrated by Alejandro Rodriguez.

www.ingramcontent.com/pod-product-compliance
Lightning Source LLC
Chambersburg PA
CBHW051953210526
45473CB00024B/2241